SEARCH
BOX BED

SEARCH
BOX BED

Darryl Whetter

Palimpsest Press
1171 Eastlawn Ave.
Windsor, Ontario. N8S 3J1
www.palimpsestpress.ca

Book and cover design by Dawn Kresan. Typeset in Adobe Garamond Pro, and printed offset on Rolland Zephyr Laid at Coach House Printing in Ontario, Canada. Edited by Jim Johnstone.

Palimpsest Press would like to thank the Canada Council for the Arts, and the Ontario Arts Council for their support of our publishing program. We also acknowledge the assistance of the Government of Ontario through the Ontario Book Publishing Tax Credit.

Library and Archives Canada Cataloguing in Publication

Whetter, Darryl, 1971–, author
    Search box bed / Darryl Whetter.

Poems. Issued in print and electronic formats.
ISBN 978-1-926794-37-2 (softcover)
ISBN 978-1-926794-44-0 (PDF)

    I. Title.

PS8595.H387S33 2017   C811'.6   C2016-908116-8
                                               C2016-908117-6

à Gisèle.
restes toujours, ma belle,
dans mes bras et ma bouche,
mon lit et ma vie

Sex is what you can get. For some people, most people, it's the most important thing they can get without being born rich or smart or stealing. This is what life can give you that's equal to others or better, even, that you don't have to go to college six years to get. And it's not religion and it's not science but you can explore it and learn things about yourself.

—DON DELILLO

The thing about love is that we come alive in bodies not our own.

—COLUM MCCANN

I. "NOT YOUR FATHER'S *PLAYBOY*"

II. THE SECRET MUSEUM

III. THE RABBLE

I. "NOT YOUR FATHER'S *PLAYBOY*"

At peak time, Xvideos might burst to 1,000 Gbps (1Tbps) or more. To put this into perspective, there's only about 15Tbps of connectivity between London and New York.

—SEBASTIAN ANTHONY

SEARCH STRING

fill the tiny
unmade bed of the search box.
Google, Google, on the wall,
who's the (where's the)
_____est of them all?
metadata and your Sunday afternoon incantation
trip the wires of smut taxonomy

the backrooms of 80s video stores,
with their saloon doors and fingered
cassettes, still cast wide nets

> *A Midsummer Night's Cream*
> *Cumalot*
> *The Joy Suck Club*

mass appeal marketing
before the mouse-over margins
became central,
online algorithms matchmaking
matchmaking
making kink matches

Victorian England covered
supple mahogany shanks and oak
ankles turned too well,
held furniture legs too suggestive
while cradling the first big porn wave.
well-thumbed French postcards
frills on stockinged stills, apple cheeks
suddenly everywhere
in the *camera ubiquita*

PORN

every cave painting has its arcing horn
and smeared curves. the stretched,
frozen hunger of unsmiling mouths
in Peruvian sculpture. Narcissus
reaching to stroke his own water,
rotund Venus of Willendorf
the Belladonna of her day.
stiff Victorian photographs captured
the penny-eyed dead, grey war
and fluffed bloomers. germy metropolitan
cinemas preceded blue-washed living
rooms, moans in our flicker walled
caves. the first comic books,
Tijuana bibles, shot more than superheroes.
the coward porn of glossy swimsuit
editions tucked in the whistling
letter-carrier's chapped hands

THE EXTINCTION

of female pubic hair
was never Tim Berners-Lee's intention

not just photogenic
gender camp alopecia
or the new low
in the slutty arms race,
this decade's tramp-stamp tattoo,
the will she or won't she,
but brokered self-delight

doubly naked, even young renters
can enjoy a home-owner's pride,
rolling up the carpet, exposing the fresh
grain of the sanded floor.
meet the market-day grin
of a poulterer with pungent thumbs.
before the hidden itch
of this hidden itch

folds of softest kid
the smiling, daily obscenity
of her pleated velour.
that stretched, sans-serif **M**
mantra, moan
mmm-hmmm

less
so very much
more

POST RAPE

by their posts
may you know them. seething
friends, cousins and office mates. invaded
assaulted, tugging cardigan sleeves over blazing
wrist burns, bruised chests and the buried
testosterone manipulations, the stubbled grins,
comments and texts. that prize
of all available limbs

we all know. statistically,
secretly then actually, the furious
women exiled to life after no. refugees
from stop and decency thrust
into predation by the leering
thieves of happiness we don't
know that we know

slideshow trauma they can't
turn off. the clatter between frames, the slashed
white bulb. night yanks and rayon fists, tugs
and such dissolution. familiar sounds
smugly rewritten, the snarl of a cold
brass zipper undoing denim.
the curse of texture, bra hooks you worry
can never be workaday
or tender again in the endless, terrible
rattle of that oh so hetero-
homophone. the calls
of refusal and knowledge too similar
in the dark

NIPPLE CLIPS ON AMAZON

the world's largest bazaar
hawks baby wipes alongside
bullets and butt plugs to target
you tip to tail. e-anonymity spares
the gum-chewers in customer service
tirades from the pant-suited
confronting their first strap-on,
all that prosthetic love
and necessity. no fallen soldiers
work security with their flashlights
to keep the boys from the fleshlights
and mid-aisle lube fights.
One-Click™ Midas knows how keenly
we await drone delivery
of our non-drone desires

CAM GIRL SIGNS OFF

pants, for a start, those profligate
pockets, all that smooth
warmth and support. the self-
entrepuppeteer thumbs down the bedroom
thermostat, slides into more than twenty
square inches of slashed
or cupped satin. de-sequin and
return to laundry-room cotton, quotidian denim.
now only socks
attend the discalced foot. pad
around the unseen, unsold
rooms of condo or house, this mortgaged sprawl
after the waitress years, the negligent
landlords

the peeled wink of the cam's green
light, more drag strip hurl
than eye of horny Sauron, a private laser pointer
secretly illuminates savings account and pre-paid
pre-school fees, not yet burning off the censure
of family reunions or adoption applications
but still catching a reliable car
bartered on castaway men,
oarlocks creaking in their subscriber lifeboats,
splashed and desperate
for the sweeping beam
of your afternoon lighthouse

UNPOSTED

blew his brother
needs cunt
black cock NOW
wonders if they bathe
wetter if I'm used
do they always have to
            fucking cry
suck harder when I cheat
only way to shut her up
spread and busy
            for the gang
her sister
            in the ass
two different
            women a day
            men together
I'll stop mansplaining
            when you stop needing me to
am I marrying him or just
            someone like him
            anyone
the redundancy of all this
            hate sex
naked with a stranger
            on my period
must love anal
unforgettable girth
a burka
            worn then raised

my friend's smooth
          bursting son
rougher in the one night's
          pretty mouth
swallowed 'til engagement
pregnant. all that
          in case of emergency glass
          already broken
such boys
unlock me

SEXTING

not how you first
wanted my thumbs,
or where. rarely a star attraction,
the foot soldier of the hand
promoted to scribe, chronicler,
an unlikely Cyrano this ungainly
evolutionary triumph still looks simian
yet holds court, sends
downstairs up, the mad
woman of the digital basement
spilling her diary in the new
ecstasy of fumbling

we've got each other
reaching, picking up the second
gigaprocessor soupcan, this private
Enigma machine of little mystery. sans serif
form still dictates content. type back
past email to the bullet
brevity of telegrams. stack
this suggestive ladder and scroll.
choose (y)our own adventure.
tap more than *Send*
as autocomplete finishes the phrase
if not the feeling

LOVES KIDS AND ANIMALS

your profile
in profile.
when did the adults
get struck off your love list?

paws and fur not a difficult
pause in the conversation. an audience
of tiny conscripts, the juice
stained mouths and harried crumbs.
enter the hacktivists of honesty:
loves a slow munch and a naked cock
thicker than a drain pipe, buried
full-octave hands and masquerading
need for nobility

loves hiking, camping and the outdoors
on Facebook. or if owning
half the gear counts. that one time
by the roiling ocean
with the taut hoodie,
and the selfie

BITS, NOT ATOMS

newspapers once shaped a world.
walnut radio turned a blind eye to illiteracy.
all those lips in silent movies
just chewing, chewing, chewing
quick worms.
TV finally cleared a place
in your voyeur's blue living room

all media and genres fuse
though not nakedly. the Net's pulsing reach
borrowed from radio and TV.
waves, not things, slipped past novels
in mortuary warehouses jolting upright
at the paint cans of film
thumped down in urban delivery

not the atomy 80s thing
            Be kind: Rewind!
nor the timed spigot of the airwaves
but the collective
shimmering dream
as peer to peer became
leer to leer
in the smartphone samizdat

THE CANADIAN AUTHORS MEET
TO WATCH PORN, NOT MMA

cage-match martial arts, sure,
but the country's largest newspaper
will never cover poets
gathered to watch porn

master's grads dial down coliseum thumbs
in book-lined living rooms
dispatching the blood-goateed
and wince-ribbed while cradling craft beer
beneath a buzz cut portrait of Georges St-Pierre

I grew up watching facials
with my dad.
Porn is a demotic art.
Bukakke satisfies
my reptile brain.
Mmmm, I'd step into that cage
of five rigid cocks

acceptable death cult residue.
broken noses, knuckle-sawed teeth, the aging
black boxer's palsy and stammer, the smashed
football knees riding beneath concussion helmets.
all suitable network fare, snack worthy,
clan time. meanwhile the gift
exchange of orgasm, the potlatch of the lap,
stays censored, mute, or taboo

A DICTIONARY OF SHAKESPEARE'S SEXUAL PUNS

1.

the crown jewel of English literature
is one filthy mother-fucker.
tosses a wink (and catches a coin)
with every rod, purse, staff, scabbard
and flower. an all holes bard
who knows a cigar
is never just a cigar

2.

the velvet leaves,
the trumpet to the morn

behold the happy wedding torch
and know against the blown rose
may they stop their nose

3.

the codpiece hustler spoke truth
to the power of the species
before the mutton-chopped Bowdler
robbed his grave (and purse)
mowing the plays with a forester's greed
while other 'gentlemen scholars' kept priapic
Pompeii artifacts and *I Modi* prints (those *Ways*)
locked in the Secretum, the Secret Museum
we all already know

ANTI-VAXXERS

the QWERTY keyboard, ghost of that iron
arachnid marionettist, was designed to slow the type
we now race to deliver. tomorrow,
as tomorrow, will always surprise

at *le* CERN, that molecular
machine in a mountain,
Tim Berners-Lee (reluctant porn king) hustled data
to chase the charming quarks.
hence, this Web

of information and misinformation, the accelerating
acceleration where typing became publishing,
irony met conspiracy and the images assumed,
the clashing graphs, marching tables, the flung gaze
of electron microscopes, uncovered
older intentions. every new lens eventually
prefers the timeless exposures

ignorance is never as deadly
as vain, self-motivated ignorance
enter a virgin (or paradise), cure HIV *(or existence).*
prefer purchased lies about autism,
enzyme-this, mercury-that, for their counterfeit
egalitarianism, the glowing confidence that your mouse
makes you another doctor, that your dusty, incomplete
or expensive BA makes you a tablet epidemiologist
and immunity
is oppression

anti-vaxxers may not know much
about science, but they sure
know what they like

FOLKSONOMY

If metadata is information about information, then meta-metadata is information about the information of information.
—U.S. PATENT

to classify is to know

chart and place
not just the scurrying
creatures of swamp, savannah and museum

but gauzy information, the churn
of abstract need

tag: a verb swatted
from the playground to the hurtling
subway cars of graffiti

label the grim
or smiling crowd then unleash
the comment feeds

touch (there you go)
and smear the video glow

SODIUM PENTOTHAL PERSONAL

extraordinary soul seeks same.
and fuck toy
cock soldier, puppet, replacement.
sparring partner, chef and sous-.
(fellow) actor, critic and character
co-authored in this hushed
theatre of shrinking privacy.
every smile, blush and prong
pings out a hidden sonar,
cell towers old and new
lovers those missing links,
amalgams of IPA love, my cloudy
bitter romantic past, present
yet banished regardless of the room.
the echo come of now and then
now, again. a key to a lock I've made
and inherited, sprung and marred
   all those
   fingers before you

PILLOW BOOK

blazing red and as compact
as your heart, shifting
from your bedside
table to mine. a thin
ribboned bookmark sifts
fantasy and commandment
in (and for) two different hands.
stop shaving here (fragrant grotto)
start there

a conditional travel guide
a second finger when X,
plead, repeatedly, when Y

lists of you are
and you have, please do. lasting
ledger for the legerdemain.
promptbook, recipes, (half-)fiction,
rape me. may I
rape you

quotation marks, those handcuffs of type, scripting
speech and speaker

II. THE SECRET MUSEUM

Even so, we have taken all the prudential measures applicable to such a collection of engravings and text. We have endeavoured to make its reading inaccessible, so to speak, to poorly educated persons, as well as to those whose sex and age forbid any exception to the laws of decency and modesty. With this end in mind, we have done our best to regard each of the objects we have had to describe from an exclusively archaeological and scientific point of view. It has been our intention to remain calm and serious throughout. In the exercise of this holy office, the man of science must neither blush nor smile. We have looked upon our statues as an anatomist contemplates his cadavers.

—M.L. BARRÉ, *Le Musée Secret*, 1877

YOGA

sexercise. not tantric marathons but daily
unconsummated orgies in expensive clothes.
now that lingerie is cheap the ostentatious curves
are yogic, every studio a rapper's choreographed dream:
upper middle class asses
up, faces down. bent reversing and candescent
in a heaving room

where else can men learn to last without whiskey.
each *ujjayi* breath a shaggy swimmer
kick-turning off one end or another. stitch an engorged
nostril into each thigh, dip the velvet
lungs into legs that will never feel longer

open and stretch the body entire, twist
with a gentler high curve ball
or Cossack's swung cutlass. thrust and unfurl
what you have and what you want
in the flush

THAT SOUTHERN KISS

late 17th cent.: from Latin, literally 'sheath, scabbard,'
which is also the source of the word vanilla.

her salt lick, the muscled
cave marbled with nerves
incubates a signature taste
a tongueprint of diet, health and concern
clouding a moss-sizzle scent
huffed to a dark whooze
before the coral
inner sanctum

the tender button, that key
left above the door.
evolution's nub
of pure pleasure, a blissed pet's
chew-marked toy. mouthpiece
for searing brass, unearthed
Rosetta stone for her other
mother tongue

HERE AT THE MIC

fellatio for a happy fella.
find the hidden
Z-dimension of your lips, their rubber
window gasket. all the collagen
and cinnamon polish, the painted
readiness for this plunging
audition, service, gobbling
reclamation

start with the eyes. telegraph
where you're going and why,
flash me wanton gems and map
a trajectory of slop

the head, the Rome of the man,
leads every road of his body.
spill wet ink down the abdominal ledger
or linger-nibble at the box-corner hips,
antipodal arrival always welcome,
spelunkers make speed-dial

a notoriously difficult instrument
but sweet music for its master,
sound me from my lowest note
to the top of my compass.
a graduated cylinder
of challenges fore, middle and aft,
Mahler's orchestration of lip, tongue and—
thank you—a squirt cushion of throat.
inhale to blur my out from your in

while a U-boat captain barks *Dive! Dive!*
crushing decibars mount with every plunge
as you pump the handle
of your own saliva well and ready
or crumple an invitation
to this wet party's after-
party

in a life without certainty
at least you know
when he's had a good time

PACKING AWAY SEX

a long-distance relationship, that
sexual early retirement, banishes
love's little prostheses. lube
just another pharmacy third-string
rolling around with expired prescriptions
fallen eyelashes and ineffectual antihistamines.
butt plugs and blindfolds
as seasonal as skis,
back-drawered and dust-furred
for this dull
aching
slip from your arms

UGLY UNDERWEAR

check out these checked,
dotted or floral
ambassadors of entropy.
freeloaders in a three-pack,
the weak point of the triangle,
agents provocateurs for planned obsolescence

mumderwear or dad's mantle,
elasticized proof of an inner life,
certainly an inner
inner circle.
monogamy's homely flag
fluttering in a Tuesday breeze

THONGS

finally, book design
that favours the back,
a shallow river
covering the valley floor.
a lonely jib sail
fluttering free of the main

as if a skeleton
flew out of its bird,
a quick migration
from runways to Sears to middle school.
a lean, panting arrival
of backbone and breast feathers

minimalism writ small.
that bisector strip echoing
the spine in miniature
exposing nearly all
yet still inciting
total sedition,
silk deposition

BEURRE, BEURRE ET ENCORE PLUS BEURRE

run the whole hand over plenty,
a wall of ass,
opposite the familiar
neat fit.
paint on a larger canvas,
have it all
enveloped

enjoy the excess. screw efficiency
and try that full-sized
car you've always eyed

your hands have clocked the hours
in the body's gallery, know
the utterly unmuscled breast,
prized sculpture of fat,
and finally extrapolate.
a billboard of softness, heavy
cream all over, flavour
spread round hips and down
generous thighs.
a queening post gels the widest
possible electrodes to spark
that current and demands both hands
clutch and stretch
at the infinite

CONDOMS

some version of your fingers
still remembers being too young
to knot your own balloon
as you tie off another
sausage casing. the medical
tang and texture

an ancient (and tepid) inner border.
more than just mummies
get wrapped in Egyptian hieroglyphs.
many an uncrooked staff stands cloaked
among the loincloths. snout-to-tail European butchers
winked and repurposed the slick viscera
of this international citizen

Casanova's beloved *English raincoat*
was actually dangled above Italy's boot
by countryman Gabriello Fallopio
(expert on the lay
of the reproductive land).
the Marquis de Sade was nothing
without his *Venetian skins*. the thin
double agent masqueraded as
les redingotes d'Angleterre
on one side of the Channel
and a *French letter* on the other

taut, translucent nylon tugged over the angry
convenience store leer of a late-night
stick-up man

THE PILL

And every life became
A brilliant breaking of the bank
—PHILIP LARKIN

the most exciting shell and pee game
in five billion years. Larkin's late-game invention,
evolution's whinnying refutation, an immaculate
misconception. progesterone counterfeits ovulation
to bend the starting pistol-shot toward a finish-line for one.
sash the breasts with the taut tape
of triumph

genes and jeans dragged
through a wet
hormonal con
looking for a happy fix.
the best crotches of a generation
gobbling up control

cellular intimacy, the original tuck and swab,
a better cry and rattle. exemption songs. play
but don't pay. daily immunity
dotting her tongue, the quick
pencil eraser of the species.
her morning smile
easy sleep and
bless this mess

STRAIGHT FROM THE AIRPORT

the arrivals gate a bath
of photographic fixer, uselessly transparent
until your bowsprit smile flashes the page.
enamel gratitude and just one
flicker of uncertainty emerge entirely unSkyped

us again beneath your sheath
of canned germs, every recycled
high-altitude cough woven into hair
I sweep aside for rediscovery

prodigal flesh after pixelled weeks—
each tongue a team member
and slick opponent. envelope lips
carry greeting and challenge.
prison-break mouths

after the eyes and scouting fingers,
four helpless nostrils
inhale the true union,
each pried animal waft
both shocking and familiar,
les pieds des notre Dieu.
finally these furlough crotches
do more than sit in the chair
of spectator
director
mourner

THE SEX ED WE'LL NEVER OFFER

sexual pleasure, the one subject
all students would enjoy, an early
double concentration

more than the mechanical engineer's Tab A
and (under-stimulated) Slot B
or Mr. History and Ms. Biology,
the chalk-coughing tweed and organ-rich
exploded diagram of dissection
barely coming together to warn:
> the Hep A handshake, the cloaked
> sleeper cells of chlamydia.
> herpes more common
> than a European kiss

a good visiting nurse gets rich
chuckles with gloves, welding goggles, a condom
and a banana, a fun house unfurling. still,
no one teaches pleasure

bureaucrats with dental care and good tires
tick off disease, pregnancy, condoms a token how-to
then banish life's strongest desire to learn,
leave us to the chance chain of our individual lovers
the isolation of closed-door labs. Google exiles stumble
through rites of erotic passage.
early anal forever painal

tell them how much a helping hand
can help. teach them all her single button
doubles as *finish*
and *more*

LOVE IN A DOUBLE KAYAK

A divorce: *kayak-guide slang for a tandem or two-person kayak.*

i.

a shared, horizontal spine
moulded seamless, the taffied
ribs of our composite body
briefly but indisputably afloat,
moving as we make it.
every tremor and swell of Fundy's excess
our pulse in hard plastic

my favourite human bar none
            and, I pray, yours
buoyed up by
                  so much
and before   more

an Atlantic bar harbour,
a nearly unique natural lagoon,
the salty *tableau vivant* of our resilient cottage.
kindled clapboarded home
of souls (if not paycheques), paint-peeling sentry
to a bi-daily bay, the reliable damp arrival
and departure of salt. gurgling, dynamic
deliquescent sculpture of arousal,
energy and ease

ii.

every love is a tidal bay.
the safe shores, the footprint
beaches best for photos,
necessary for launching, your stern paddle
necessarily grabbing before mine.
leave the tranquil, slack corners without friction
head instead to the reliable mouth,
the suck of the most powerful
tide on the planet frothing
over slick grey rock and a many
splashed shore

drawn into the channel, aloft and just a little
endangered. the liquid borderland,
a bay within a bay
        self within a self.
a draining, wet bridge between two cleft ridges
of tossed grey rock, half-submerged walls
unseen by any mason yet still
precision-fit by wave and tide.
beside and now behind us
the paddle grows quietly muscled
and the green
depth beneath broadens, solidifies,
nudges our float

iii.
normally we prefer the fifth-gear fight
out the narrow channel, water-slide
and wind sprint, scuffed red plastic us
cursed and blessed in the sloshing
millions of litres. the whole tipped planet
pouring in then out our lapis
rock-ringed cauldron.
the tidal bay a tangy stretch
before and after full-throated,
deep-bellied Fundy

not, for this late August sunset, the full
oceanic bay and its insatiable hunger
demanding every inch.
lever past the tug, sweep
the restored, polymer fins,
pry ourselves forward and glide,
this once, 'round to the still side
the floating
road less travelled

iv.
shelter isn't always easy and all
stillness wants to be observation.
our suspended vantage, a magical chance
in the smeared magic-light
to feel one water and watch another.
the slack calm beneath us and,
howling and racing beyond the breakwater,
the tide and all appetites

skim a brief paddle,
you one minute, me the next,
to anchor us in water so still
so mirroring, that caught pollen and white,
errant feathers, scoops of puff and pluck,
pull back in our fractioned
footnote of tide while just half
a boat-length beyond us the waves
commit their gurgling *hara-kiri*
against rocks they'll only meet once.
cobra-hooded with colour
in these connected dots of me, you,
weeping breakwater and self-annihilating wave,
the long, turbulent trough of Fundy,
leaden landing strip for this setting
late-summer sun. that inveterate orange projectionist
lifts the bay's workaday blue
into the aged moss green of a flung wave's crest
or silvers its daguerreotype foam, hammering the slate

into greyscale as we parse
you, me, and us
amidst the familiar
float and roar

TOYS

the shop, the wall
of third-party cock.
need it. need it. got it. got it.
thick, compact, long and
who could possibly?
supplementary or complementary,
wingman or designated hitter
(curved just so)

prosthetic, tireless and utterly
undemanding. humming servants
with buttons external
and in

butterfly, rabbit and dolphin,
her silicone bestiary. all that
engineered gear inverting
the gender clichés. her tool
to his text. magazines then Web reels
of brokerage and splash, Mr. Narrative,
Mr. Character 'n Scene, while she charges pleasure
she can always boil clean

REALLY JUST TWO WORDS

transcend class:
wrong hole

CHEATING

car-crash fast flung squealing metal to the witnesses
while inside the spin you still understand
exactly what's happening

self-realization or self-sabotage a drugless high
but still an addiction that could get you evicted
every pricked pore doubles as eye nostril mouth
fingertip entire hotel-room synaesthesia flash-mouthing up your body
down mine a charged shroud far more arousing than black
suits and garters coming so hard you teleport inside your own soul

far more than hair in each sure fist the lash
against in-laws halved bills the snores you unleash or endure
the smear of who you are and must be

ruin greasing the rails an undressed rehearsal for suicide
and the utter animal flattery of loyalty newly laid

III. THE RABBLE

All these hierarchies of sexual value—religious, psychiatric, and popular—function in much the same ways as do ideological systems of racism, ethnocentrism, and religious chauvinism. They rationalize the well-being of the sexually privileged and the adversity of the sexual rabble.

—GAYLE RUBIN in *The Feminist Porn Book*

SPANK ME

free from the tyranny
of hole one, two or three.
give me that starburst kiss
and map a wincing
ring road round the whole haunch.
garland my rump, this thickest meat.
each delicious whack
tugs me back from volume and insertion
to flower-press into the crimson
second skin of curved hurt.
rumbling Baghdad, blitzed London, the amber flare
and night shudder of our combat sky

glove my hair tight in your fist
to parse the *pliant* in *compliance.*
ribbon and cat-pull the entire
arm of dark speed, rubber fling elbow,
wrist, then sparking finger
through the amped nodes.
lash velocity red and blossom
this necessary
play

MONOGAMISH

The key to marriage, she concluded, was just
not to take the thing too personally.
—LORRIE MOORE

admire her appetite
and admit that an evening
holds nothing to a decade.
send his steam
temporarily elsewhere

courageous gift, brave demand.
zipper licence, mouth warrant, the honest
karma of the crotch, a well-dressed
vacation from exclusivity.
soul, bed, and mouth
contain multitudes

new life in the little death,
fresh tugs at belts, buttons,
expectations and the settled years, a heave-
ing, heel drumming horizontal confession.
me too
as honest as
I do

THE BONUS TUNNEL

the final intimacy
a second, more tender virginity. so lovely
to be so careful again. relax in pure
adult confidence yet repeat the teen
game of (half) inches

a gopher hole's dun collar,
the inverse, antipodean mouth
ingesting for a change. a snug
bassline melody

so close, yet so different, a younger
messier sibling with a shared
bedroom wall. knowledge overheard
and overhead. the deep

and endless expansion, the tightest
you'll ever hold me

MOMMY

indulgent succour
the sop, slip, and tuck
of knowing fingers.
the veteran of mess
and surrender. all this
insistent gravity

shush, shush. I know.
where and how and here, filling
a mouth while filled again
ever so briefly

DADDY

knows what you show him
and must punish
comes into your room at night
has your hair in his fist
owns and gives you presents

knows what you must at night
comes into your hair presents
and gives you punish
has your room in his fist
him you own show

at night in your fist know
comes into your punish room
what you hair give
must in his owns has
shows you present him

owns what you room him
comes into your must fist
and hair shows
presents what you night punish
has your gives in his know

SIR, MADAM, SIR!

There's not a lot you can't do to a man if
you have his hard dick in your other hand.
—MISTRESS MATISSE

you've always known
your dick's a double agent, that all swords
are sellswords. stage half a mutiny
and put that fickle rise
to rented use. hire the heels
in tall boots to extract
your own admissions,
school you in hurt.
dog-pack epistemology
and the shorn tender shown

Punish(me)nt. opened in winces,
welt-banished in my own body, scurrying
between your crop's fence post whacks. the crimped,
arcing lobster muscles in my lower back.
banded and caged. each shoulder a trussed roast,
hoisted arms lattice my ribs,
for a fast ivy of climbing pain. flicked
leather kisses

each slap sparks a gap. scream and turn
against your ridiculous scrotum,
the rodent purse. agree the nailed rat hide
must consent and beg the clipped
walnut ridges you fix

you've never won this grapple
without knowing the shape, stretch and heft
of loss. speak it now
from your animal corner,
stronger/weaker, more/less,
no/yes

THE RED BADGE OF COURAGE

a painter in her time
moon swept and redefining
bloodlust. a vegetarian's ethical source
and copper font, the cycling
Ferris wheel of her ferrous weep

refuse downtime and fly
below the dumb radar of conception.
passport, prophecy and curse
written monthly down thigh,
throat or chin, red
fairground tickets pressed to a greedy palm,
this inked bounty of the body's accounting

spread a dark towel
and collusion
for her smear and holy
blood without a wound

TAKE IT LIKE A MAN.COM

a word
of sisterly advice:
peg him.
turn the tables with tech

your rented reach. six
to twelve tubular inches
of unbending silicone
snug in a proud harness

aimed at the buried treasure of his prostate,
that plum, that VLT button
hording its jackpot trill

flip your fluency
with the handles of the hips, repeatedly
take delivery
and whinnied assent. secure
his firm backing

GOÛT DE TERROIR

lick her gold clean to recognize
the marinade of your days, this splashed
addiction to tin. cedar,
edam and the very definition
of salt. the olfactory tideline
of her water, a ripping river
with a source you can find

a racehorse power
no man can attain. buzzing
signature of inner heat.
another sluiced bridge
slung from skin to skin.
ammonia yanks,
drawstring nostrils,
the desert thirst
you stretch of my chest, back
and throat. yellow,
prison confessions
forced from a tongue

DIY.COM/FECALTRANSPLANT

I miss my pre-internet brain.
—DOUGLAS COUPLAND

with ten bacterial cells
for every one human
we live in minority parliaments
not autonomous bodies. squatters
in our own genetic homes, enabled by,
not just enduring, the assembled
powerful rabble

to immunologist and GI-specialist, *high diversity*
resides in the gut, that labour pool
of temporary foreign workers
forever doing our dirty work

sterile guts in the womb, long and coiled
tabula rasa before the bacteria-
wash of birth. life's friendly strangers
and occasional enemies. as variable as our souls
and arguably inseparable

with a stained library
Good Gut or quiet Google how-to
Necessary Materials   and our outnumbered soldiers,
latex gloves, sev. pairs   lovers can now fuse even more
whirl a   *thrift store blender*
tepid saline spread that old   *brown towel*
hook a high hose and release
into another

A HOME OF ONE'S OWN

living alone, the divorce
of the twenty-first century, common
yet still a neighbourhood nod, shadows
of hushed *hows* and *whys*
when we already know

you say *bathroom door*,
I say *oblong robe hook*
(that room with a sudden view).
me, myself and I the only resentment
in every mess. rumpled
floorboard underwear, proprietary flags.
the tumbleweeds of half-balled socks.
privacy curated snugly in sparse fridges.
sex finally a figurative sport, periodic scoreboards
ever readng *Home* and *Visitor*

city blocks, warrens of wired solitude
with everyone clicking away. come
but don't live with me, and be my love
and we will some
pleasures prove

ACKNOWLEDGMENTS

Earlier versions of some poems appear in *The Malahat Review, ARC, Prairie Fire, Calliope, Event,* various editions of *The Fiddlehead,* as well as the anthology *Canadian Ginger.*

The following studies were helpful: *The Feminist Porn Book: The Politics of Producing Pleasure* (Eds. Tristan Taormino et al.); Walter Kendrick's *The Secret Museum: Pornography in Modern Culture*; Aine Collier's *The Humble Little Condom: A History*; Fenton Bailey and Randy Barbato's six-part documentary *Pornography: The Secret History of Civilization*; Laura Kipnis's *Bound and Gagged: Pornography and the Politics of Fantasy in America* and *The Porning of America*, by Professors Carmine Sarracino and Kevin M. Scott. Sebastian Anthony's article "Just How Big Are Porn Sites?" in *Extreme Tech* details the enormity of erotic content online ("30% of the total data transferred across the internet"). The title "Not your Father's *Playboy*" is transposed from Gail Dines's 2010 article in *Counterpunch*. The title "Bits, not Atoms" is taken from former MIT Media Lab Director Nicholas Negroponte's book *Being Digital.* A March 2014 Toronto Star article on MMA viewing by Nathan Whitlock prompted a poem. Dan Savage coined the term "monogamish," and an episode of his podcast *The Savage Lovecast* contains Mistress Matisse's sage advice. French poet Léon-Paul Fargue originally described the delicious stink of soft cheeses as *les pieds des Dieu.* Bill Hicks has a joke.

AUTHOR BIO

Darryl Whetter is a short-story writer, novelist, poet, critic and professor. His debut collection of stories, *A Sharp Tooth in the Fur*, was a *Globe and Mail* Top 100 Books. His debut book of poems, *Origins*, received a starred review from *Quill & Quire*. A former CBC Radio books panellist, he reviews for *The Globe and Mail* and *The National Post*. A resident of Church Point, Nova Scotia, he has been a Creative Writing professor at four different Canadian universities. Currently, he is a visiting professor in Singapore, where he is the inaugural director of the first Creative Writing MA program in Southeast Asia.